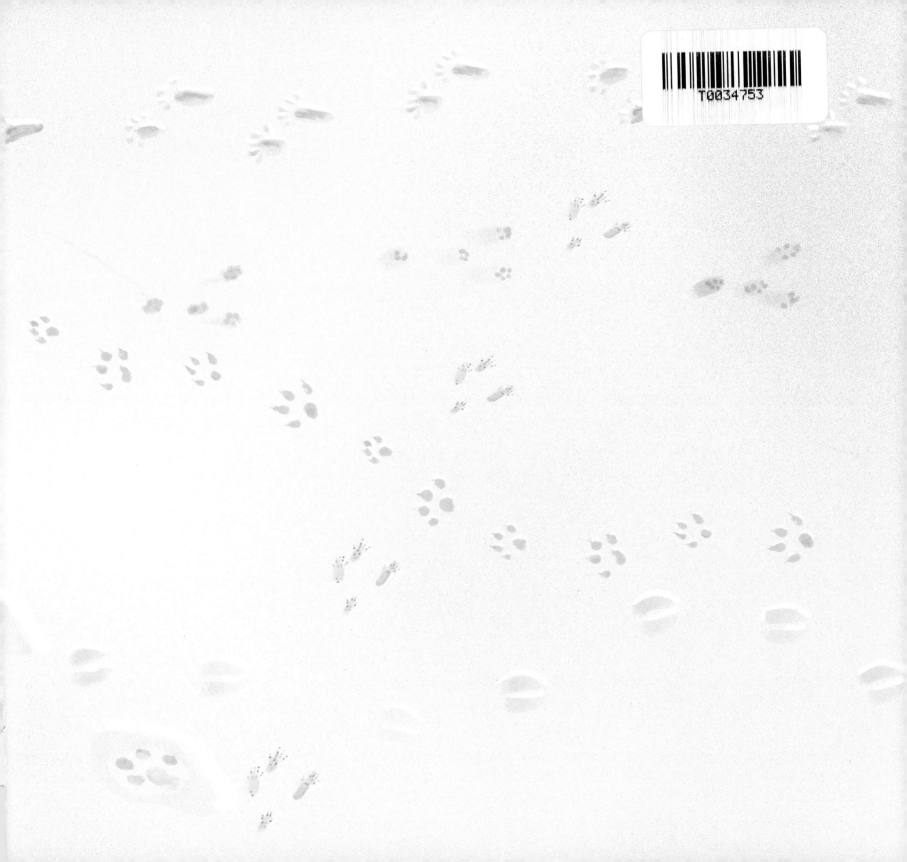

Hiders Seekers Finders Keepers

How Animals Adapt in Winter

Written by Jessica Kulekjian
Illustrated by Salini Perera

KIDS CAN PRESS

When days grow short,
flowers fade
and colors crumple to the ground ...

all the hiders hide.

As autumn weather cools and food becomes harder to find, many animals look for a place to rest for the winter.

They're under cover,

Wood frogs have a chilly twist on winter survival. They tuck themselves into logs or leaf piles and practically freeze solid! When warmer days return, they defrost and hop back to life.

Eastern box turtles dig underground burrows and wait out winter in *brumation* (similar to hibernation). They lower their heart rate to five to ten beats per minute and stop breathing completely! Instead, they soak in oxygen through their skin.

burrowed deep ...

Chipmunks slow down their bodily functions (such as their heartbeat and breathing). This slumbery state is called *hibernation*.

Bumblebee colonies die out in winter, except for the queen bees, who enter a state of rest called *diapause* (the insect version of hibernation). When the queens emerge in the spring, they lay eggs and start entirely new colonies.

and snug inside dens.

When **black bears** hibernate, they enter an inactive state called *torpor*. During this deep rest, they can go up to 100 days without a meal. In periods of wakefulness, mama bears give birth and nurse their cubs in the coziness of their hidden winter homes.

Some swirl and curl up where nobody can see.

Snakes hide in dens, caves or tree stumps during brumation.

Snails seal off the entrance to their shell with mucus to prevent drying out.

Hundreds
huddle
in
stillness ...

side
by
side.

Some species of
ladybugs spend the winter
packed together in large colonies.
They remain in diapause until
small insects called *aphids* — their
favorite food — return. Other
ladybug species stay active
through winter. They seek
out warm places, sometimes
even people's homes!

Carpenter ants produce a substance called *glycerol* that prevents them from freezing. They hide in trees or logs and stay inactive (unless they are in someone's toasty house!) until the weather warms.

And while the hiders hide ...

the seekers seek.

Many creatures migrate to a new home in search of warmer temperatures and better food sources. Scientists believe the decreasing daylight in autumn is a signal that it's time to go.

Arrows cross the clouds, pointing
their way toward a new home.

Canada geese fly in V formations, playing follow-the-leader as they head south for the winter. Each adult bird takes turns leading the flock. *Honk!*

Hooves thunder over hills,
through water and into valleys.

Elk, pronghorn antelope and mule deer move to areas where the snow isn't as deep and food is easier to find.

Wings scribble across the skyline.

Eastern North American monarch butterflies may flutter close to 4800 km (3000 mi.) to get to the mountains in Mexico where they spend the winter in oyamel fir trees (also known as sacred firs). The migrating generation is sometimes called the "super generation." It takes only one generation to migrate to Mexico, but several to make it back to Canada and the northern part of the United States.

Thousands chase tomorrow ...

one

by

one.

Ruby-throated hummingbirds seek new territory once the nectar and insects they eat dwindle in the winter. They can fly up to 37 km (23 mi.) in a day and typically travel alone.

Green darner dragonflies migrate south in winter. Scientists only recently discovered their migration routes because the dragonflies don't stick together for their entire journey, so they can be difficult to track.

While the hiders hide, and the seekers seek ...

the finders keep.

Some creatures have adaptations that help them tolerate and survive harsh environmental changes.

They keep warm bundled in coats,

White-tailed deer and **red foxes** grow winter fur that keeps them extra warm.

keep full with buried treasures ...

In the fall, **mice, gray jays** and some **squirrels** bury meals such as nuts and seeds to eat later in the winter.

and keep close enough to kiss.

Female **red squirrels** cuddle up with their families to keep warm.

Great horned owls take over abandoned nests. Then, they lay eggs and begin raising their young in late winter.

Millions make their path ...

step

by

step.

Tracks in the snow
are clues about which animals
have passed by. Deer, moose, coyotes
and bobcats leave zigzag tracks of
prints in shapes that match their feet.
Foxes leave behind prints in a straight
line. Rabbits and squirrels make
four prints in a pattern that matches
the way they bound ahead.
Lynx prints are shaped like
ice-cream cones.

Snowshoe hares and **snowshoe lynx** have large padded paws that make it easy to travel on top of the snow.

When the sky spills on the ground,
the hiders hide,
the seekers seek
and the finders keep until …

the sunshine warms again.

Track Guide

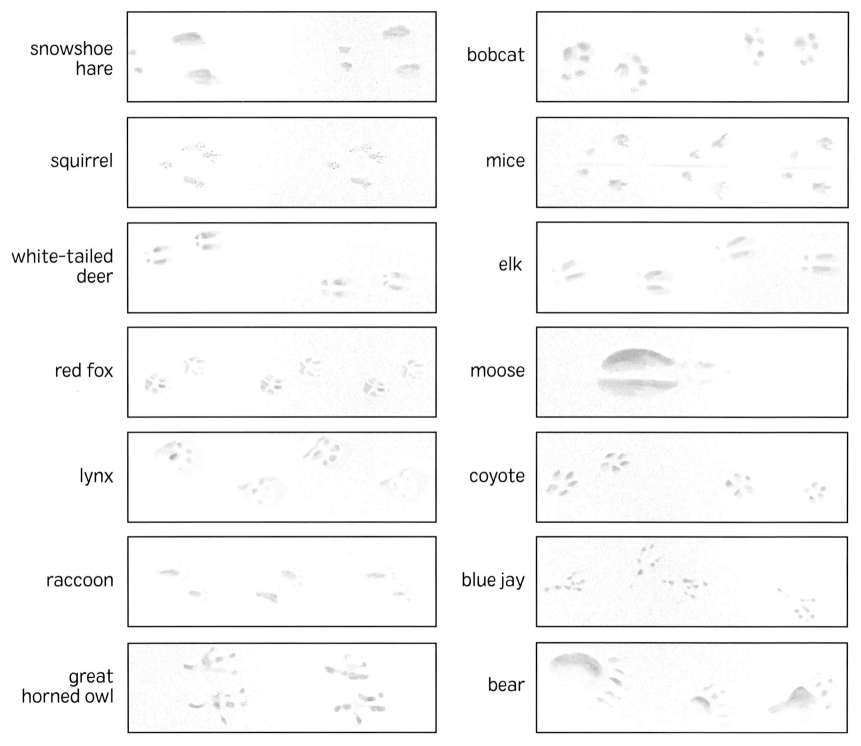

snowshoe hare

squirrel

white-tailed deer

red fox

lynx

raccoon

great horned owl

bobcat

mice

elk

moose

coyote

blue jay

bear

Author's Note

When you explore your neighborhood, what changes do you notice?

My kids and their questions inspired this story. During our neighborhood walks, we observed wildlife changes throughout the seasons and our curiosity grew. We wondered about the bird species that came and went and why all the frogs disappeared. These questions led us to books, websites and films, which revealed more fascinating discoveries about how animals adapt in winter.

Every creature has a different way of preparing for and surviving winter. Some hibernate, others migrate and some tolerate the changes by adapting with their environment. *Hibernation* helps an animal conserve food and energy by slowing down and resting. Animals have different ways of hibernating. *Torpor* is a short-term physical state an animal can enter to cope with intense cold. In torpor, an animal's metabolism, breathing, temperature and heart rate all slow down. Cold-blooded animals, such as reptiles and amphibians, enter a hibernation-like state called *brumation*. When insects become inactive for the winter, they actually pause their development and wait until temperatures warm and their food becomes available again. This is called *diapause*.

Meanwhile, migrating animals seek out warmer weather and food sources in new locations. Some even raise their young before heading back. Animals that don't hibernate or migrate adapt so that they can tolerate winter. They might grow a warmer coat of fur, huddle up to share body heat or change their diet to match what is available.

How do you adapt in winter?

If you'd like more information, here are some resources to get you started.

Books:

Atkins, Marcie Flinchum. *Wait, Rest, Pause: Dormancy in Nature*. Minneapolis, MN: Millbrook Press, 2020.

Davies, Monika, and Romina Martí. *How Far Home? Animal Migrations*. Mankato, MN: Amicus Ink, 2019.

Hickman, Pamela, and Carolyn Gavin. *Nature All Around: Bugs*. Toronto, ON: Kids Can Press, 2019.

Salas, Laura Purdie, and Claudine Gévry. *Snack, Snooze, Skedaddle: How Animals Get Ready for Winter*. Minneapolis, MN: Millbrook Press, 2019.

Unwin, Mike, and Jenni Desmond. *Migration: Incredible Animal Journeys*. New York, NY: Bloomsbury Children's Books, 2019.

Films:

Nichols, Jenny and Joe Riis, dirs. *Elk River*. United States: Pongo Media and National Geographic Short Film Showcase, 2017. VOD.

Perrin, Jacques Cluzaud, and Michel Debats, dirs. *Winged Migration*. France: BAC Films, 2001. VOD.

Websites:

https://fws.gov/story/phenomenal-monarch-migration

https://hummingbirdcentral.com/hummingbird-migration.htm

https://livescience.com/32812-why-do-bird-flocks-move-in-unison.html

https://nationalforests.org/blog/do-bears-really-hibernate

https://washingtonpost.com/science/2018/12/21/theres-huge-hidden-migration-america-dragonflies/

For the noticers, wonderers and dreamers,
who are imagining a better world for us all — J.K.

For my father, Srilal — S.P.

Acknowledgments

Many thanks to the following individuals who enriched this project by sharing their expertise:
Julie Constable, PhD, Department of Biology, California State University, Fresno; Mike Hadden,
Operations Manager and Regional Bird Specialist, Rentokil North America; and Jay Kaplan,
Director of Roaring Brook Nature Center, Canton, Connecticut.

Published in Canada and the U.S. by Kids Can Press Ltd.
25 Dockside Drive, Toronto, ON M5A 0B5

Kids Can Press is a Corus Entertainment Inc. company
www.kidscanpress.com

The artwork in this book was rendered digitally.
The text is set in Colby.

Edited by Kathleen Keenan
Designed by Barb Kelly

Printed and bound in Buji, Shenzhen, China,
in 2/2023 by WKT Company

CM 22 0 9 8 7 6 5 4 3 2

FSC MIX
Packaging from responsible sources
FSC® C010256

Library and Archives Canada Cataloguing in Publication

Title: Hiders seekers finders keepers : how animals adapt in winter /
written by Jessica Kulekjian; illustrated by Salini Perera.
Names: Kulekjian, Jessica, author. | Perera, Salini, 1986- illustrator.
Identifiers: Canadiana 20210360135 | ISBN 9781525304859 (hardcover)
Subjets: LCSH: Animals — Wintering — Juvenile literature. | LCSH: Animals —
Adaptation — Juvenile literature. | LCSH: Winter — Juvenile literature.
Classification: LCC QL753 .K85 2022 | DDC j591.56 — dc23

Kids Can Press gratefully acknowledges that the land on which our office is located is the traditional
territory of many nations, including the Mississaugas of the Credit, the Anishnabeg, the Chippewa,
the Haudenosaunee and the Wendat peoples, and is now home to many diverse
First Nations, Inuit and Métis peoples.

We thank the Government of Ontario, through Ontario Creates; the Ontario Arts Council; the Canada
Council for the Arts; and the Government of Canada for supporting our publishing activity.

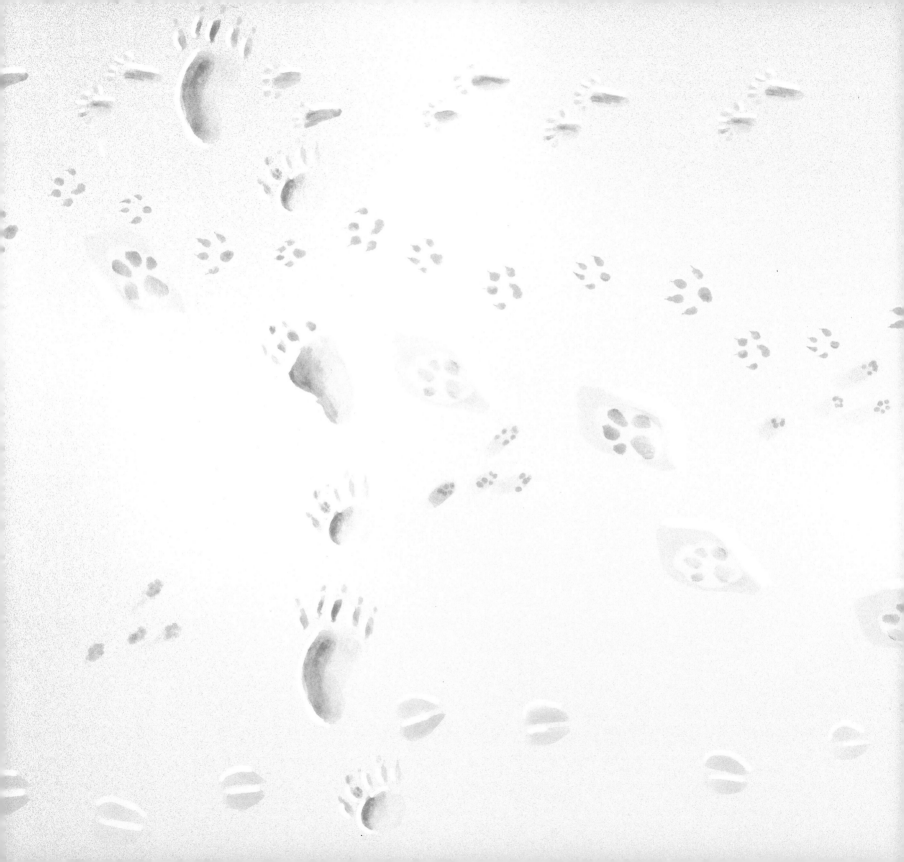